THE DOVE WHO BECAME *Human*

THE DOVE WHO BECAME *Human*

DYLAN MITCHELL

PALMETTO
PUBLISHING
Charleston, SC
www.PalmettoPublishing.com

Copyright © 2024 by Dylan Mitchell

All rights reserved

No portion of this book may be reproduced, stored in a retrieval system, or transmitted in any form by any means–electronic, mechanical, photocopy, recording, or other–except for brief quotations in printed reviews, without prior permission of the author.

Paperback ISBN: 9798822962040
eBook ISBN: 9798822962057

To the hands that guided my work,
To my forgotten loves in the blustering wind,
To my friends who listened to my work with kindness,
To my father who has given me the tools I need to find my path,
To my mother who has made me into the one I must be to walk that path,
To my brother who knows me more fully
than any other human being on this earth,
And to every lonely heart traversing a lonely street
that I have not yet had the chance to meet,

Take a breath.
This book is yours
as much as it is mine.

Contents

To Fly 1
    Future 3
    My Fine Amor 4
    Reason Needed 5
    There Is No Glass 6
    The Truth of the Sphere 7
    Bravery 8
    Purple 9
    To the Anticipated Ones 11
    Visitor 12
    I 13
    A Child's Grasp 14

To Fall 15
    Questioning 17
    Heartbeat 18
    Do As You Do 19
    Asunder 20
    Further 21
    Below 22
    My Name is The Sun 23
    Clouds at Night 24
    Descending Upwards 25
    Pace 27

To Land 29
    Drought 31
    Storm 32
    Echo 33

    Goodbye Summer 34

    Windows 35

    Resurgence 37

    Fifth Day of Rain 38

    Misty Mornings 39

    Paradoxical Heart 40

To Walk 41

    Seasons 43

    Late Night 44

    Warmth 46

    Take the Crown 47

    Rolling Waves 48

    Hello Again 49

    The Frozen City 50

    Wayward 51

To Be 53

    Will You Speak My Name? 55

    Sonnet of Peace 56

    Sacred Taciturnity 57

    Dear Comfort, ... 58

    Little World 60

    What I Write 61

    Becoming 63

About the Author 64

# To Fly

Future

The child,
he will achieve great things.
He will paint the canvas of life,
taking the brush and tracing meaning
through his love.

He will be admired,
but it will not matter to him,
for he is his work.
He lives for beauty,
like that of the stars he rests beneath.

He is powerful,
but more fragile still,
and although he may change the world,
a simple gust of wind
could blow him down.

My Fine Amor

Oh, cry no more my fine amor,
though sky may fall beside the door.

A dry encore, malign and sore.
Life goes awry, to live is war.

I swore I caught your eye before.
I'll fly for you to see my core.

Goodbyes galore to sighs of yore.
For you, my heart and soul can soar.

Reason Needed

Why do we love?
Is it to convince ourselves
that we have a reason to be?
Perhaps a plan for the final words upon our lips?

Do we crave the cure
to some chronic anhedonia?
Or perhaps we simply want to be warm at night.
The night is cold, after all.

Do we miss a morning's calm,
the way it used to be?
Or is it that we stride braver
knowing that a net hangs below the wire?

Why do we love?
Go find out.

There Is No Glass

Ripples trembling in a glass,
a medium that light can pass,
but certainty is poison gas,
and so I break the cup.

Water spreads upon the ground
with shards of glassware scattered 'round,
and so I gather, not a sound,
to slowly pick them up.

One by one, I stack them high,
a bridge that spans from land to sky.
With endless beauty, I could cry.
The world is born anew.

Gone are thoughts in glass confined.
The shattered pieces of my mind
have formed these prisms intertwined,
with colors in my view.

The Truth of the Sphere

                        All

            love   love

          that   that

      lives   lives

          in   in

            this   this

                    world,

Dylan Mitchell

Bravery

The sultry sun arising in the east,
I watch it as it falls toward the sky.
There may not be a meaning in the least,
but I may yet believe that we can try.

And, like a knight who charges 'cross the hill,
protecting purpose from the clawing dark,
I will believe that life has greater will
than days of nothing full when we embark.

You see the dangers that we face ahead,
but we are stronger still than dread's malaise.
We are as one, as living and as dead,
but death will quiver at the banner's raise.

Your valor sees the worth within your heart.
By living, you become the greatest art.

Purple

The sweltering rays were abated only by the cool mist
which I tried so desperately to avoid.
Do you know how hard it is to get spray paint out of your clothes?
My laughter and hers wove together,
washing over the sound of the creaking wooden patio.
I grasped the weapon of mass inconvenience in my hand,
just as she did,
and we completely forgot about the spare canvas that we'd found
in the stone-cut basement.
Another volley of arcing colors,
ringing into the summer air
like cool ocean brine.
My mouth was tired from smiling,
my legs were tired from running,
and we made a truce that could not be spoken due to the
mutual catching of breath.
We sat on the edge of the porch.
Then, with the unmistakable pop of the cap,
I felt my hand go cold.

A somber April day in a riverside town almost two years before then,
and a year before our time apart.
We sat upon the stone-cut walkway with our backs to an iron fence
as the misting turned into a drizzle.
Do I reach for her hand?
The sound of distant tides crashing against the rocks mirrored
my heartbeat,

resolute and rhythmic in my chest.
It was raining now,
and the water was beginning to weigh down our purple hoodies.
The rain was cool on the top of my hand
as my fingers interlocked with hers
for the first time.

Purple.
I looked at my newly painted hand as she began to laugh.
The sweltering rays were abated only by the cool mist
which I'd failed so tragically to avoid.
She leaned into me and I put my arm around her as we looked upon our barely painted canvas.

"So, what do we put on there next?"

To the Anticipated Ones

We all are born from broken songs
into a sea of war,
so here we are to right the wrongs
of those who came before.

Are we the ones to mend the seams
and build the earth to last,
or are we all but ravaged dreams
and specters of the past?

There is no room for pain or doubt,
the time to move is here,
to change the world within, without.
The need for us is clear.

Although the road is perilous,
We know that we will rise.
We see that life was made for us
to mend with open eyes.

Dylan Mitchell

Visitor

Funny crow, you funny thing,
hello to you today.
What black feathers on your wing
that carried you astray.

What a mind behind the eyes
that knows the worldly tricks.
What adventure in your soul
that carries you betwixt.

Look upon me, tilted head,
and know me by my face.
Do you know the ink I spread
that celebrates your grace?

Funny crow, you funny thing,
hello to you today.
What black feathers on your wing
that carry you away.

I

I am simply a complex simpleton.

I have never gone a day without dreading my final day.

I feel things deeply, but my face deceives itself.

I have never turned down a friend in need of my blood.

I regret all that I do for myself but have no plans to stop.

I fear the present as much as I fear the future.

I have never taken a walk without deciding on its purpose.

I have never decided on my purpose without taking a walk.

A Child's Grasp

Reach with all your might.

Feel your fingers graze the sea.

You will soon hold Earth.

To Fall

Questioning

Breathless beauty of the sky,
blustering serenity.
Watching heaven's iris die.
How could this be?

Stoic strength of oak and ash,
in the glade of ancient few,
tethered down by flame and gash.
What withered you?

River fierce with flow of earth,
endless stream from start to start.
Portent true of true rebirth.
Where is your heart?

Ever-genius, ever-kind,
we were made to be as one.
Splintered, leave the world behind.
What have we done?

Heartbeat

…
Quiet.
Quiet.
This is it.
Minutes remain.
I'm terrified and tired.
My family came so far for me,
They're all here now.
Just relax.
Time slides away.
Calm down.
Quiet.
…
Quiet.
Is this it?
Will I die here?
What about my dreams?
The people I love will miss me.
Just close your eyes.
Try smiling.
What if it's empty?
Nothingness?
Quiet.
…
…
.

Do As You Do

The words will barely reach my hands,
and so I write from fear and dreadful sight.
I walk outside your faerie lands
and feel the gloaming kiss of dredging night.

In knowing aught of hearts aglow,
I've lost the knowledge of my life before.
A hundred thousand years ago,
It's said that I was capable of more.

My dulcet torment, take your blade
and kiss me as it pierces through my soul.
A paradise you thus forbade,
your frightful majesty is true control.

I beg to lay my head on thee,
your loving hands around my neck and face.
I know we weren't meant to be,
but I will always flee to your embrace.

Asunder

I tread across an empty place,
a nation torn asunder.
The sky is filled with haunting grace
from hollow, rolling thunder.

I feel the cold of death's embrace,
the fear we've fallen under.
Will spirits fade without a trace?
I cannot help but wonder.

Birds will soar at dizzy heights,
with none to see them thrive.
Brittle land of dimming lights
the dark will soon arrive.

We have lost the will to fight,
as sorrows intertwine.
Hope is but a parasite,
so loss becomes divine.

Further

Soaring through the sky with you,
directed by the plans we drew,
but as they failed, we veered askew,
so from the heavens, we withdrew.

Trudging on into the blue,
turned to grey and made untrue.
A gloom by torn maps, missing glue,
We knew that gruesome terror only grew.
Snap.

                    A flickering star, guiding the way. It does not matter;
                        North, East, South, West, none can exist anymore.
                              Only I and the deepest stars align ourselves
                                          at the borderline of infinity.

                                                    Reach out.

                                          Further.

                            Further.

               Further.

A gloom by torn maps.

Below

The moonlight bathes this silent land.
I walk alone and think.
The world around me falls to sand.
I find my place and sink.

It's nights like these that sting like love.
Goodbye is no hello.
I see the hollow sky above,
the lonely earth below.

I am slipping away,
slipping beneath.
Help me.
Don't listen to me.

Getting
Over
Never
Ends,

Always
Walk
After
You.

The unknown below us is manifest fear,
but could it be better than what we have here?

My Name is The Sun

Spark in the night
and I'm due to take flight,
as I kindle the flame
'til it's boundless and bright.
My name is the sun
and so how can it be,
that in consummate love,
I still long for the sea?

My embers caress
and they roll down my dress,
and yet drowning them somehow
is what seems the best,
so I run to the shore,
doomed to burn evermore,
for I never shall reach
what my heart has in store.

Clouds at Night

Clouds at night,
devoid of light,
a hollow sight across the rift.

Summer air,
perhaps I'm there,
but who knows where the winds shall lift?

Am I late?
With terror great,
I face my fate, concise and swift.

Nothing bound,
for I have found,
though on the ground, we are adrift.

Descending Upwards

Staring at the ceiling of my ground-floor apartment,
tight and confined,
I feel the air enter and exit my lungs
with its abiding truth,
fueling my eyes to love further
the thousand hues of beige.
The color becomes itself in a beautiful crescendo
of modest peace.
No taste could be sweeter.

Sitting at a table,
sipping my bitter wine and wearing a smile
given only by words.
My eyes trudge across the beautiful cloth
and silver.
I find my will as I raise my glass
to a hundred more nights
of wayward thoughts
and noncommittal breaths.

Dylan Mitchell

Staring at the towering mosaic behind the altar,
its images of the sky's collision with the land:
the joy,
the love,
the faith.
I taste each of their blades
cutting through my throat
as I pray to that which steals my voice
without recompense.

Standing on a balcony
in my robe and crown,
buckling under tenebrous chains.
From above,
I look down on the stagnant lights
with disaffectedly mishopeful eyes,
eyes that have seen better
and felt less.
I mourn unparalleled beauty.

Pace

Subject of the heart,

wreathed in flames of frenzied love.

Wisdom in the ash.

To Land

Drought

The world has been aflame,
death and life adorning the curbs
in this concrete utopia
of immaculate illusion.

The marks of life
settled in aridity
remain,
like echoes in an endless cave.

We are nearly drowning.
We are burning, drowning.

Thunder rolls over the distant skyline.
It's about time we had some rain.

Storm

A lifetime from a summer breeze,
and broken on the land.
I strain to rise from back to knees,
then further 'til I stand.

A hurricane of broken dreams,
the eye is closed to me.
I pledge to hear the silent screams
and work to set them free.

What good am I to those in pain
if I am missing form?
I write my truth to block the rain
with words that pierce the storm.

My joy and love I wish to stay,
my anguish I rescind.
The vile me is swept away,
a whisper on the wind.

Echo

My love, I'd give the world if I could stay,   Stay
and how it grieves my heart to be away.   away.

My soul is made for you, as yours or not,   Not
and cold will be the day when I've forgot.   forgot.

Though nevermore are you and I to be,   Be
I've bound my flesh in ink to ne'er be free.   free.

With voices lost in darkness I will write.   Write
You told me once that I could be your light.   light.

I wonder what your smiling face would say   Say
If you could see the man I am today.   today.

I will always love you.   You.

Goodbye Summer

I taste the breeze, I hear the call,
I feel the cooling air of fall.
I smell the rain within the glen
and wish to see you once again.
I long to fade within the days
where winds permit that subtle haze
and spirits trickle from the pen.
I wish to see you once again.

I feel the crushing weight of all,
so unaware of where and when,
but thoughts of you will smiles raise.
I wish to see you once again.

Windows

A tasseled cap hanging from the door,
a testament to work and achievement,
swaying back and forth in the wind.

Swaying with the wind on a midnight beach,
the lights of the boardwalk fading into oblivion,
a broken heart in my chest.

My heart beating quicker in my chest,
dancing the night away,
looking into her eyes as I see love.

Learning what love is for the first time,
what it means to give oneself to another,
but not understanding how.

Not understanding the world,
a young, lonely, strange child,
serenaded by a mechanical lullaby.

A song sung with tender love,
slowly rocking a son to fleeting rest,
laid inside of a baby-blue crib.

A baby-blue crib, fresh and new,
designated for one yet to arrive,
standing patiently by a window.

Gazing through a series of windows,
each a shade of what has come before,
a thousand precious memories
just out of sight.

Resurgence

The deep and shallow intertwine.

I weep and watch the gallows dine.

As waves align, I brave the brine,

defy my grave to raise a shrine.

A flux of vital lies resign.

The current churns the coarse to fine.

Divorce the source of force malign.

I'm hollow, check my vital sign.

Fifth Day of Rain

Lugubrious dawn,
see the fathoms in the lawn.
What reason could there be to leave the bed?

Yet another day,
begging but to waste away,
and, like a lover, longing to be dead.

Do you hear the sound?
Gently growing from the ground,
and pushing you to live beyond your head.

Grass will soon be tall,
flourishing by evenfall,
reminding us that we can be misled.

Misty Mornings

Voices lost within the mist,
wayward still I see you roam.
Lonely, waning, evening-kissed,
find your heart and make it home.

Dreams of past will conflagrate
in the flames of winding time.
What is there to consecrate
if we burn a world sublime?

What is there that lies above?
What is there that lies below?
Keep your virtue, little dove,
love it more than you can know.

Fate would see us overrun,
ev'ry story bittersweet.
Angel of the morning sun,
sweep me off my mortal feet.

Paradoxical Heart

Ever is it true

that the heart will scream in ink

to thrive in silence.

To Walk

Seasons

Thinking of a life,
thinking of a ring.
Moving fast, forget the past.
Loving life in spring.

Know I wasn't strong,
know I wasn't wise.
I will stay, I heard you say.
Screaming summer lies.

Taking on the wind,
taking on the rain.
Hellish chill, I'm lying still.
Feeling autumn pain.

Nothing to be done,
nothing to be lost.
One by one, we learn to run.
Scraping winter frost.

Late Night

Tethered.
Waning, impermanent,
the night is small here.
Surrounded by cliffs,
yet forced to run
nonetheless.
Past trees and brooks,
to darkness I am carried,
to the night I return.
It welcomes me.
A glimmer of something above.

At the edge of sight, the true forms of the sky.

Weaving galaxies.

Burning novas.

Arcing asteroids

Thoughts become starlight.

Body remains,
but what could we become if it didn't?

Worlds beginning and ending.

                                            The sun rises, and all is erased,
                        but I remember.

Dylan Mitchell

Warmth

The tempest forged in hellish view,
which came without a warning,
erased our night, and split us true.
You left my sight by morning.

My legs grew weary in the frost,
my thoughts of you were prison.
My body cold, my spirit lost,
my terror had arisen.

There was no solace to contrive,
my moments passed as ages.
I learned the facts of death alive.
My wisdom shamed the sages.

I'm loathe to leave your warmth behind,
but still the bells are ringing.
I journey with you in my mind
and find a new beginning.

Take the Crown

I greet my grief and own the mess,
a seed of fake compliance.

My sweet relief is loneliness.
I bleed in sacred silence.

In waking coup, above the skies,
I cease this blackened weather.

I break the glue of lovely lies.
I piece me back together.

Rolling Waves

Make me whole, vibrant blue of loving sea,

    there are few who can be your gentle tide.

        Far from me, I confide, I cannot flow,

            petrified in the glow of future's grip.

                Could I go on a ship and sail away?

                    Could I clip through the day with quiet mind?

                        By the bay, leave behind my passion's graves,

                            just to find rolling waves within my soul.

Hello Again

I cannot tell you what we swore,
I cannot see tomorrow.
I cannot feel you anymore,
for I have crafted sorrow.

I dwell within a vibrant cage
with bars of iridescence.
No lilting love nor holy rage,
no life within my essence.

But now you reach your hand to me,
a long-forgotten heart.
Last horizon that I see,
but with me from the start.

I yearn to know your soul, my sweet,
embrace your silhouette.
I feel your hand upon my cheek.
"You will become me yet".

The Frozen City

In a station, underground,
ice tracked in and slowly melting,
a son and his mother wait for their train.
The child sees its approach
and watches the conductor with wonder.
When can we be who we want to be?

In a quiet, secluded park,
snowbanks framing the path ahead,
a person walks with their lover.
Their hands become one, swinging lightly.
They catch each other's eyes and smile.
How can we be so happy?

In a high, glass building,
the winter wind howling,
a person in white enters again.
The diagnosis is given,
and breath is stolen from the room.
Why are we so temporary?

In a low, stone building,
the frost embracing its windows,
a poet's pen scrawls their mind.
With isolated will,
the culmination of pain is born.
Cherish what you have.

Wayward

Although the night chills,

the sun won't hide forever.

I am the morning.

To Be

Will You Speak My Name?

Grasping toward empty air,
I drift across the brink.
Misty visions that you wear,
a visage in a blink.

Though the ocean waves will tear,
love my pen and time's affair.
Know me more and feel me there.
I never want to sink.

Know me more and feel me there.
I never want to sink.

Sonnet of Peace

I walk along the road with eyes aglow,
the trees of vibrant green before my gaze.
The dragonflies are buzzing to and fro,
the birds let out a song of bygone days.

The cars that hum and whir are born of breeze;
with cooling gusts, they venerate my stride.
For once, my steps are met with only ease.
This isn't what I know, I must confide.

I never thought I'd see the world as new,
a place where I may peace and wonder feel,
where ev'ry breath I take is pure and true,
where honesty has made my spirit real.

I stop and close my eyes. I feel the sun.
In ev'ry moment, life has just begun.

Sacred Taciturnity

Driving down a seaside highway,
sand eclipsing road ahead.
Holy Oceanic Gateway,
show the place for which I bled.

Resplendent beach with astral sand,
surfer's soul within a god.
A board obtained from Neverland.
Whisper how the world is flawed.

I'm left with but the land he gave,
watching as he takes a dive.
Repentance carried on a wave.
Now's his time to come alive.

A secret land for him alone,
sacred taciturnity.
Invincible yet danger-prone,
gliding to eternity.

Dear Comfort,

So many look to you across this barren field of truth,
grasping for salvation,
their waning hearts beating slower.
Slower.
They hallow thy name,
unsure if you are our progenitor,
or our child.

The solace of mind you have given,
this gift of vanquished impermanence,
has been received many times over without true knowledge.
In the face of vacuous, endless nothing,
a hollow promise is our only light.
The match that we struck
and forgot.

You have not given me your name, nor have I let you,
but so many have before.
In opulent sanctity,
illuminated by the chromatic stories of those long-passed.
On silent knees and with clasped hands,
they receive that which came from nothing.
I watch.

And so, I write to you,
my most treasured ash in the wind of my mind,
I remember the days when I could see your kingdom,
when I sang with the faith of believers.
Oh, how I would receive your name if I could accept you,
but I cannot.
I love you, but my belief could never be yours.

Through struggle and strife,
we kindle a flame all our own,
warming ourselves by this fire.
The spirit I trust is that of humanity.
The end I see is the slowing of my mortal heart.
This is not comfort,
This is purpose.
I can find God enough in that.

I still treasure the lessons that you taught me.
From you, I learned that I could live without you.

Little World

Pebble in a sunny field,
framed around by wild weald.
I can see what once appealed
beneath your little shade.

Light cascading warm and wide,
reaching out to ev'ry side,
but still, in darkness, they abide,
within the world you made.

Pebble, pebble, let them go
and loose the lost from down below,
to sun, to rain, to sleet and snow,
and make them unafraid.

Little world they leave behind,
the sun's embrace will treat them kind,
but still may come a day they find
the shadow's serenade.

What I Write

My poetry is a message I haven't read,
something that I send myself
in unfamiliar handwriting
to learn about my fear.

My poetry is a terror,
something that I must vanquish
with rhythmic, delicate splashes
of ink's revelation.

My poetry is a storm,
the final moments of war.
The settling dust
whispers my meaning on its way home.
On its way home.

My poetry is the eldest of my youth,
the culmination,
the finale of a story
still in its third chapter.
The ending before it's over.

Stories do not have to fill their pages.

Becoming

Lovely little dove,

do not fear the fall below.

You will soar again.

About the Author

Dylan Mitchell, a Philadelphia native, is a therapist with a masters in applied positive psychology from the Philadelphia College of Osteopathic Medicine. He honed his literary prowess studying psychology and creative writing at Temple University. Dylan finds solace in poetry, often utilizing it as a unique storytelling mechanic in his favorite pastime, Dungeons and Dragons. His writing is deeply influenced by his personal experiences, familial relationships, and his active involvement in the LGBTQIA+ community. Dylan is also parent to a sweet but generally unskilled cat named May. His book, The Dove That Became Human, echoes his diverse life experiences and his passion for empathy and understanding.

Milton Keynes UK
Ingram Content Group UK Ltd.
UKHW020826231024
450026UK00004B/420